DISAPPEARING, INC.

DISAPPEARING, INC.

POEMS BY **BRANDON AMICO**

ISBN: 978-1-64204-924-4
Library of Congress Control Number: 2018958458
Austin, TX

Disappearing, Inc.
2019, Brandon Amico

goldwake.com

CONTENTS

For Catherine

CUSTOMER LOYALTY PROGRAM

The opposite of not existing
is shopping. I am less the name
given me than my portion
of our nation's GDP. Student loan
interest rates and 401(k) projections
tangle on a graph, spurring one another
toward climax. I am my credit score
(777, which means I can afford
to gamble) by way of most common
denominator: the easiest consistent definition
for those who pass me on the street,
who sneeze into my collar, who walk
their dogs like their own sovereign nations.
The main export of dogs is love, because
that's all we'll take from them. I withhold.
I charitable contribution. I put into
a MEEK fund so I inherit whatever's left
when the wars are done. Take
the whips and minimum gags allowed
by law and say thank you, chew
on the inside of my cheek. I am alive
when restrained, know my body
by what it pushes up against.
I am putting in my dues, stretching
my life out till next week's paycheck,
and the next; withhold a little bit
every other Thursday until
refund time, that time of year
all the S&M shops dream of, for we buy
new, plastic-smelling gags, we buy leather,
our own handcuffs. Will the nation
spoon us after? Do we need
SSN safewords? Are we expected to speak
with all this debt in our mouths, and what
would we say if it's removed?

A QUESTION

How long between aphelion and the chrysanthemum's full wingspan?
How many bees are there in a day? We're working, we're working on

shrinking the orbit, increasing the spin, we're developing the technology
to speak to the non-technology. Your imagination still works—imperfect.

Derivative, your heart still thuds, and your tongue still good as the ear
it reaches, the lips it parts—how many beats in a minute, per scene,

per day? And per curve? *Apogee*, the waves harmonize; *perigee*,
they break. Aphelion, the flowers bide beneath the frost,

fibrous knots of subconscious, waiting to be called back—and they will.
Seasons: the original robocall. How many between bees and no bees?

ANTIPHONY

For every new marriage, there is an equal and opposite divorce.
The Bad Stork brings text messages, 1 a.m. phone calls. I'll never admit it
but yes, I saw a ghost. I can't show you, because I didn't inhale it—
can one be haunted by absence? The assured sleep well at night,
whereas I crack jokes to leaven my worry in the blare of midmorning,
even as this gets me disapproving looks from the Serious Adults
at the hearing; their ties stiffen audibly. Here are my lungs
as ghost-proof, my spleen, all my Bad Humor. What was it
they said about denial, that it's nine-tenths of the law? Scrape off
the solemnity, the tar from my mother's Bad Habits—both put up
in the lungs' lining, and maybe the ghost will be there too, that which we
dress in internal weather, storm of capillaries blue to red,
microtransactions swelling with each breath. My hour with the therapist
is not practice for a stand-up career, I am told. Am I to go into my father's
line of business? How unemployed is one considered at twelve? Keep
looking for work, something beyond this call-and-response
of living, the punch-line of another's joke leaving scars on a timecard.
Exhalations: if we laugh, we're not to be taken seriously, we're not
believed, we're in contempt—but I want to be taken
alive and kicking the bones that Bad leaves on my doorstep;
portending is so boring. It's hard, when one already knows
the end to all the stories, not to pull a god from the machines we make
of our faces. To speak into the silence, the life support. I stockpile jokes
in my own eulogy, testimonies, vows. At birth, my wailing
surprised no one more than myself.

THE FEAR

The War on Christmas is purely economic—
cranberry paint for the more graphic Christ
statues, dabbed on cable news lenses. Created,
as wars are, by those invested in creation
and ongoing. Those with a stake
in the holly. The falling action—snow,
dollar bills summoned out from under mattresses.
The climax of cash register bells caroling,
the ladling of soup from bowl to vat, the steam—
from the gutters, from the peppermint
coffee, from the running back's helmet-less
scalp, the fog flickering like smoke in a hearth,
a cherished logo in the heart of every home
and across midfield. A bear would eat her young
to deny a predator the privilege, I am reminded
by the figures winking at me from my Coke can.
There's no sorrow we can't overcome
by drowning it in eggnog, a drink
for every day of the week, of the season, Black
Friday, Elegy for Those Trampled (when our
TVs observe a moment of muting
in their honor), Cyber Monday, Green
Throughsday. I am not alone in the brotherhood
of failing to be better; of owning
good intentions and being buried under
the interest they accrue. Water wasted
when ice cubes are dashed from the
finished cup. The fear that comes
appended with due dates. The fear
we wear on a chain, hang from
the fireplace, the doorframes, on the fridge
and the blue spruce which we deny
well into Spring must ever be thrown out.

A NEW GUN FOLDS UP
TO LOOK JUST LIKE A SMARTPHONE

—Huffington Post, March 30, 2016

Gun that folds up into a teddy bear.

Gun that folds into a bottle.

Gun that folds into a dozen roses.

Gun that folds into a condolence card.

Gun that folds into a conference pass, a baseball ticket, a ticket to anywhere.

Gun that folds into your golden retriever, the usual tail wag. The jolt of electricity through the tail when you say its name.

Gun that folds into another gun.

Gun that folds into a prerogative, into an absentee ballot.

Gun that folds into a bulletproof necktie.

Gun that folds into rope.

Gun that folds into a grin without a face.

Gun that folds into legislation—folds and folds until so thick it can't physically be folded again.

Gun that guns into a fold.

Gun that folds into an opening.

Gun that folds quietly.

Gun that folds into a weather forecast, a travel agent.

Gun that folds into a car key.

Gun that folds into a door key.

Gun that folds into a body.

Gun that folds into a mirror,

that shatters.

Gun that folds into a crane, into another crane, into a history lesson.

Gun that folds into an anti-NRA sign.

Gun that folds into a picture frame.

A gun swaggers into an argument.

Gun that folds into a pen. Gun that unfolds an ink cartridge.

Gun that folds white as paper, that writes its wishes.

Gun that folds its fingers into a steeple.

Gun that folds into a pantry.

Gun that folds into a knife fight.

Gun that folds into a sitcom episode without an ending.

Gun that folds into itself, that becomes more gun.

Gun that folds in err, in human.

Gun that folds into a cell phone; gun that calls your children home.

AUGUST

O damn it, my dog dug up the lede.
I guess we should talk about existence.
No sense dallying with all this living
when dirt's seeping up from the new rug,
when the robins have fattened and don't fit
in their woodshop houses, when
the squirrels are stringy, desperate
around the limbs and stare down the hill at deer
who look back up at them and the house,
and the house cat who doesn't (yet) know
what digs behind the birch-dried tree line
foregrounding the steeple, as we don't know
can't know what perches between navel
and steeple, which is to say our crown,
our limbic nest . . . Look, I get it,
I know the laws; I will get to the Truth, will check
that box, shoot the dog who foams at mouth
and the horse that drags itself into the house
pleading, mud on hooves. What can you say
to eyes that look at you like their begetter
saw you, how would you compartmentalize
a smile refracted through another's light,
the confusion of spheres that mark our orbits
through each other? Alone our planet
turns, and elsewhere the sky churns separate;
the bowl, the pear, the dawn that burnt away the fog
and took something else with it. The cancer that hides
parenthetical, till later in the story. The reversed gasp
of that first day, and the next day, and the dog out back
with its ears down, though it did nothing wrong.
What mantel to place our anger? What walls
to build with fire in mind? Decorum seeks to marble
us all. Let us speak loudly in His house,
that He may hear it and pass along our message.

GIFT TAX

Entropy crafts us
the finest ghosts.

You live and you breathe
until you've given

all that's legally
permissible

under carbon tax
guidelines. Every hello

costs you. Each goodbye
triggers a refund

in grass whistles,
graveyard strawflowers.

Enough, implies
the lion's jaws,

bracelet-clamping
the cold wrist,

dragging us to its den.
Furnace. *Enough*

denotes finitude,
everything is enough

in a world of limited
resources. In the high court

of windows grasping
littered sun,

we swear to see
her face reflected

                              in the morning's
                              vapor, the silver,

impeccable china,
a mother

                         whose eyes would meet
                         yours in the rear-view

before checking your
seat-belt, an aunt

                              a sister whose body
                              balanced

on a beam of light,
became percentages

                         shifting, rates of survival,
                              became less and

became unlatched from time,
daughter became vessel

                              became a chrysalis
                         of untranslatable light—

grew in the final hours,
grew in the morning's

                              new color grew
                         blooming under the faces

of those leaning over
her, grew and

                                    grew until
                                  the light

was too strong and
the body, too,

                    couldn't contain it

SELF-PORTRAIT WITH ONCOMING STORM

What if there were another nor'easter like in '78
when twenty-eight inches clogged the streets, and what

if a second arrived on its heels, budgets have been slashed
and so too the plow fleets, warm-colored liquid raised

in a warm window passed on the street, toasting
the New Year's lean new budget, and this

is why I don't live farther north, the roads thinner,
colder the capillaries quicker to collapse in my fingertips,

toes blue as a storm-shook sky, one jackknifed
tractor trailer on the highway's a clot and the tissue downvein

dies, arthritic bridges handed down
piled up with snow, stuck inside and O

shit my prescription, my mortgage bill, it's only
January, downed power lines unreachable,

unplugged, and what, even with power what
about cabin fever, nights when the stars

crowd every window and mock us like giddy,
spare snowflakes, twinkling down in their arbitrary

constellations on all these parts contiguous,
more joint than solid bone, what happens when

we refuse the leave of our bodies, unable to extricate
ourselves, unable to welcome a clearness that could

settle on us, security as wind, as a solitary sound,
the earth's whispered hush, hush, sleep now,

hush, I've got you, you needn't grip so tight.

I HATE THE WEATHER CHANNEL

And Weather.com hates it
when a hurricane slices back to the ocean.
Meanwhile I, as a poet, should not hide
behind line breaks. *Why There Are No Atheists*
HERE was an actual headline on the site—
the break was all me, but that's my own
editorial responsibility to bear.
GRAPHIC: Sperm Whale EXPLODES
is another; one could, conceivably, argue that
the weather for the mites and plankton offshore
would change by an appreciable degree—
with the introduction of whale particles
into the immediate atmosphere—and thus
this article was germane
to the organization's duty. *This Toy Store*
Will Haunt Your Dreams! and while yes,
all the baubles of analytic insight and pay-per-
click return-on-investment could keep
a CEO up at night, I am haunted already.
We are enough worry without you.
This clickbait and switch, *This Python*
Ate WHAT?—yes, ate that exactly,
ate the air, the question, the hollow
of nineteen seconds wasted to fill a hole
so recently punched in the mind.
What Really Killed Cleopatra? Probably
something that fell from the sky
when she was looking
at her phone. Tell me again
about the *MONSTER Bear Captured*;
will you ship it to the circus
on the rails you've conjured
out of humidity and the internet around us
to will the storm toward the cameras
inland? *Don't Let This Happen*
to YOU you exclaimed, you demanded,
you warned, you wished.

OZONE

You can see the roots, the water they soak in. The trunk that
sentences its way up, parses branches to cover more ground. Well—
more air. The air more in a well than out is damper, brings the earth
to our nostrils. That distance is called a mountain. The difference
between *in a sense* and *in essence* is similarly wide. Further,
innocence—a gap that could fit our planet. The condensing of sentence
structure, entropy of elevator pitch. A star   burning itself away;
some just prefer to announce their combustion. A word for our falling
apart and trying to slow it down. I left my lips somewhere nearby, I'm
sure of it. Teeth in the cobwebs, *How 'bout that weather lately?* and other
kitsch in piles by the bed.   *Lately and Other Stories
in the Key of Desk Fan*, my latest collection, is unfurling toward the same
oblivion as our colloquialisms, as our veneers, as our batting and
pitching records—as the cat listening to me type, or listening
to me read, the silence of trust a kind of song. The sheet music
for the universe is written solely in rests; whole industries are built on
transcribing the noise we can't resist making. Will someone
listen for the morning with me? Burning sky, come crashing from over
the hills. Heated, order   snaps its bonds, a forest fire
east to west. The twigs crack and thud. The piano is a bomb, and each
generation reaches over the others' arms, trying to find the perfect pitch.

MUSIC VIDEO

I will buy you a cell phone the size and luster of Paris, will buy you
a plane ticket to the other side of your home. I'll buy you a proper family;
each struggle will bring us closer together and when the cats die
we'll make them into belts and the third cat will tie us together
forever. I will buy the sharp ends of your memories
so you can bury them all in your spacious yard. I'll buy you theme music,
credit-reel saxophones—I will buy you the 90s. You'll wake up
to the alarm clock's new crooning and copious sunlight, you'll remark
that this is what the 90s were actually like; the economy will hang plump
from the branches outside your window, like an island framed
that I could buy for you as well. I will buy you a sense of purpose
fulfilled, manifested, perfectly fuzzy edges, a glow
coming from the corners of every room. I will buy you
a Cold War punchline, a fact-of-the day, Bazooka Joe comic
tucked in the child's lunchbox with an ice cream sandwich melted
by noon—your mother was so excited to surprise you, to be around
to watch you grow. I will buy you a house that looks
like hers. It will have a peephole with a view of the world.
I will buy you a key for disappearing into the material around you,
for cocooning. I will buy you your mother's ashes, still
warm in the earth after twenty years.

AUDIT

Quick—do you recall everylastthing
about your mother—her favorite Beatles songs,
the brand of her jeans?   Ask not
                    what your country does

          for you,
but what it makes affordable.
Balance cost   -   benefit, review
          weight and texture,   the memory

                    a stone in the hammock
                    of your stomach, while the good
ones turn on   above you
with a zap,   a halo

of Christmas lights.   The stars
          arranged across the porch
and eaves in constellations
          of simpler

holiday visits.
                    A lamp-light
coming in from the yard,
snowfall disappearing in the denim.

THE FIRST TECHNOLOGY

I dial into a conference line on mute to feel
loneliness pinball for a time. Each mouth rests
around opinion, a fruit, teeth testing its flesh.

So many people I can go to and be alone:
every conversation a cage or key in our tradition
of toggling, editing—freedom and its decay.

Easiest when I diversify my loneliness. Invest in the
mainstream and rivers counter-currenting. Industry flows
into military, limbs preface their use. Should I speak

and dare an act of contest, risk the opening
of a door to a nectar flood and handshake-sickness.

How can I attract, write down the past? With
honeybee blood, fruits and dyes smeared on a wall.

MISSION STATEMENT

Anything that occurs is, by definition, historic.

I chartered two businesses in the course of a week
just to crash them together, see who could hold
on to the masts—in the gale of incorporation
documents and tax dodges, who would remain
to inherit the cask of an empire.

Turns out cloth was all that caught in the mast, a flag
for what—surrender? Job creation? Decency

to clothe the entry-level workers in a world decked
with entropy? Is the sky decent to rain

on the drought-stricken lands
enough to flood, to rip off
what little shrubs had splintered through
the plains surveyors read like palm lines—

should we feel grateful being consigned to one flat,
wondering what it's like to live in the apartment
across the street, to wear one's clothes
inside out for a day, buttons measuring navel to clavicle,

tag limp in our wake, pleading for warm,
gentle rain, tumble dry only, and wouldn't you know
the world continues turning, despite, the wind
carries your scent, lifts you in its jaws.

NOTHING BUT

"Where, where is the town?
Now, it's nothing but flowers"
—Talking Heads

When I became poet laureate of this corporation,
I was bestowed certain irrelevancies allowing me
to function in ways the rest of you could not.
This was necessary for my post to be wielded effectively
and not be bogged down by the need for balance
or decorum. Free from the yoke of measured competency,
I wrote first drafts in red ink. Revised my dreams
mid-yarn, bound financial reports with guitar string. Today
I'm resigning amid the shame of granting personhood
to this corporation—it is with deep regret
I report that during my tenure, all I've learned
is to say *my body* instead of *my god.* My
body, how I've changed, the shell I have made and carry
from place to place on my back. My body, the world
I live in today, full of monsoons and
car washes. I'm sorry—but when I make love now
I can't even hear the tax forms folding over,
the brackets shifting, deductibles rolling up
like camping bags. I look
at my wife's face and I see wilderness.
Untranslatable. Where is the town? Where
is my body, the convenience stores
that were cells? The body does the work of the body,
the King does the work of the sun and
the tree does the bidding of the wind,
shareholders each rustling a leaf in earnest.

DE TOROS

The carpet wears clothes
in ways I can't.

Effortlessly. Comfortably.
Without thought.

There is nothing more polite
than self-consciousness.

It appears to be a body
behind the cape. Sometimes

it is, and at times
the suit won't stop talking;

if I hold the fabric properly
I can have a whole

relationship without
opening my mouth.

Come on; it's me. English
speakers say *matador,*

leaving out *of bulls.*
How we dilute, sieve

through syllables.
How our shapes approximate

on the floor, the mannequin,
we hang ourselves

in closets every night.
I speak to the world

by walking into it. Overheard
at a funeral: it's a shame,

a damn shame, wasting a suit
by burying a man in it.

EPITHALAMIUM

The woman at the table two tables over
is planning her wedding. She says a name
then *maid of honor*—the honorable name
I recognize but cannot place;
the information, long thought to be useless,
hears its shape called for and tries to call back
from its vault. Where do you put a second
chandelier, you know, just to store it awhile?

~

Here is my heart—its second half
is studded with clock marks,
throats a menacing tick.

I stand at a summit;
does it matter the direction I step?

~

A wedding dress flipped upside down—fabric
fallen open like petals—showers ants.
Some cummerbunds are structural by design:
undone, and the metal spring can't keep the torso upright,
the head plunges down, arcs toward the ankle.

Let us dress for ceremony and its scaffolding;
to have and to hold you up.

~

I have married so many times only to lose
the ring in pockets, handkerchiefs,
sleight of hand a nervous tic I perform
without thinking. Naturally, I suspect
conspiracy: my clothes fear consummation,
resent the idea of me shedding them.

Magicked the self across mirrors
leaning into other mirrors, saw my body
as interrupting, pulled taut by light.
For my next trick, I will saw myself
in half.

For my next trick, I will need an assistant.

~

I pull chrysanthemums
from my throat, magician's
scarves, all kinds of colors
all tied together
with the word *yes*.

~

I married the wrong twin
and it stuck, I pulled off my mask
and she pulled off her mask and it all
worked out.

The little man in my chest
who pulls the gears saw his reflection
in her eyes. Shocked,
he fell from his perch and died—the floor
of the will is marble, the ceiling a rush
of flame.

~

Do you take cream in your coffee? (I do.)
Do you have room in that hat for another head? (I do.)
Do you promise to mend all guitar strings, repaint
when the barn dulls and every half century
fire off the silo like a rocket when the capricious weather
pulls your crops out on a whim? (I do.)
Even as age slaps your twined knuckles? (I do.)

~

Here is my body, take.
Here is my throat of silver,
skin brushed with oregano, thyme.

I've come from a body
swollen of fruit, take
seed I am given that anchors
me down, deep, roots me,
gift the years, here
the counting, the telling,
the always and forever take.

Until death unlaces our grasps.
Until the bright scarves like flags shed from our cuffs.
Until we lie down at the chapel of Western roads
while the sun spools off behind the glass . . .

~

I am sunk to the ankles in cake,
I did not budget for the dry cleaning,
the wax of my joints to melt like this.

I am the rice dynamite hissing
from the dove's gut, my flint tongue
saying *drink.*

~

I am lost to the patterns sewn
meticulously throughout my pockets.
Trapdoors, deeds to other tricks,
tactile illusions.

Do you give her your hand? (I do.)
And if all the light left were fallen in the ocean,
you would unmoor the rowboat and find it. (I do.)
You would feel for the boat's edges in the dark.

T-REX

Un-tasked with breath, but still taking on air
and light, and light on its feet for once—

feeling up for a jaunt to the gift shop
to buy what it thinks is a mirror.

~

And yet the spirit has no weight
to move the hull. It spills through the porous bones,

if even a thing at all, boomerang once slid from the jaw.
If it loves you, it'll come back.

~

Lights out. The guards grow beards,
lose them, grey, but every weekday morn comes the same

mellifluous light, the honeyed light that cradles
the same bony mask in its palm.

~

When you're famous, you're known for one
famous expression, encyclopedia-worthy.

The T-Rex attempts a smile for field trips
but the bones don't give; jaws remain child-sized.

~

Cannot see the plaque facing outward by its feet,
cannot speak to assumptions of temperament,

tyranny. Of all the imaginary, unmusical—
the tin box roars below at the press of a button.

~

In which the keys of the great lizard's spine
sing under the swoop of a sliding Fred Flintstone.

Nat King Cole: *But it wouldn't be make-believe
if you believed in me.* In which the dead still speak to us.

~

Now the distance from which extinct begins
its bleed into imaginary.

The mountain's relief worn down, green
fog spreading smooth. We turn away.

~

And so the lions, and so the sightless insect
that never escaped the jungle's palate, and so

the mammoth, manatee, and my heart, worked over
and remolded again, fit snug anywhere but my own chest.

~

And so the continents that, over millennia,
draw their breath then exhale. And so each morning

the bathroom light comes on and I excavate
my face, try to step backward, toward what I remember.

COMPULSION

I

You! With the pulse! Do you
have the bandwidth, do you own
a sensible pair of everyday shoes
to cross both college
and company campuses
wondering how your parents
bought a house for forty grand
at your age—are you prepared for the answer
to every question posed to parents
and politicians alike being *Jobs, jobs,
jobs*—wherefore art there only jobs?

II

Where are the art jobs? At the office party,
you must contain moral fortitude to enter
the pumpkin-decorating contest with
a plain pumpkin, labeling it *conceptual*,
leaving yourself at the mercy
of your coworkers' creativity. Do you
speak to yourself
alone at night, not knowing
which side of the argument
you want to win? If you bring
your art to work or your work to art,
you have made art work. Have you sold
out? Where will you place
the Houseplant Sonnet—is there
nothing between sellout
and starving artist? It's easier
to let go of happiness than resentment,
which is why saltiness is a natural preservative,
why the high road is freshwater
floating above while the below bitters on,

bides, and the planet tires of our gnatlike
presence. All the drinking
water left'll have salt in it
to keep, always the imperative to preserve.
All the politicians' points are wreathed
in flame and flung toward us, a baseball
sending a clear message to the batter,
but if we're not hit-by-pitch it'll be the clouds, and if
the clouds don't smother us the waves will, a salt rain
up from the earth. No matter—we'll sell out
or just learn to market better, float
on the wave of stereotype;
we've learned to ride out
what desiccates all
trying to buck the temporal, the great bull
of humanity slams its horns
into the stock exchange, the new
leaders have nukes but won't pay for
a glass case around the FIRE
button. Here the acid rain and
the brighter rain throwing shadows
that stick on walls and make
the rivers shock the seared
horses to death for seeking relief, and the humans
too, waiting
for the sky to cauterize the wound
in the air, for the earth to rise
in crystal and keep us, and
hold us tight, for this home to want us all along.

III

Make art because it syncs with our dying.
It requires our hands. Make love
because the drum insists, beats
on, wakes us in the morning says
off to the subway and prods us to
every line we're destined
to stand in, the song stays
caught in our throat and our ready

joints because no one sings
while waiting for coffee, while staring
at the text conversation and its burbling
ellipses of possibility. The ozone
doesn't sound its exit
like a stock exchange,
like a dinner bell.

ONLY 90S KIDS WILL GET THIS

Poetry tip: The most natural line breaks are achieved by positioning a drinking bird above Enter and typing normally. Stop. Rhythm, stenographer of emotion, the only perpetual force. Stop—as everything does. This is a mute point—as in, stop the program where it is, let it lie where it's laid. Our youths are unstoppable objects, hard kernels of gravity flung from our universe center. If one is to Netflix and Chill, this presupposes a volume of this phrase high enough to enter it into the cultural consciousness. See also: earworm, jingle. If we are left alone to the televisions of our youth, it is believed the 90s will repeat itself. That's just like us millennials!—leave it to our sentiment to shirk the duty of disappearance.

Elsewhere, older generations already weaponize nostalgia—there are bodies that come up when dragging the river for rocks our grandparents skipped in the 50s but, the bodies being dead, we only hear the stories of those who found them. Nothing more comforting than a border of static language, the story treading circles that become a trench, a moat. No proof of the dangers of our default if there are no words for otherness. The pundits absolve collateral damage, refuse the bird its needed momentum. The idea of the absolute, the peak that is crumbling away under millennial boots. Look for the signs of blood bleached from hands, the invocation of a glow so mesmerizing it's like looking into the sun, everything's so white.

#MOONGATE

O Harold, I'd love to go to the Springtime Ball with you, but
you have less than a hundred followers
and I'm not trying to get mixed up with some kind of monster.

Your content is lovely, truly it is, but you
need to engage with others. Where are you
when not cheering with us at the Homecoming game—
people like to know. Listen, I think the world of you.

More than the world—you hung the moon!
...but the moon is clearly straining the sky, look, just
look: it's trending. At a glance it *seemed*

to be yanking on the clouds but now there's been a poll taken
and it's decidedly doing so. We have the science, Harold.

It was a nice gesture, but maybe it's time to take it down.
Think about the kids, they might find use for it someday.
Have you thought about kids before, Harold? They're like blog posts
that walk around and edit themselves. I know,

I know; your content, Harold,
your *content!* But your platform's a mess—can't you
make it like a pop song, or use more active headlines? You know,
the kind with one half missing, the side of the moon

we don't see, so people can fill the other half in themselves?
(O, to feel the substance collect in a conversation!) If only
you could do that, you'd be the bee's knees, that is

if there were still bees. You'd be the last song on the last
songbird's tongue, right before it burst into flame.

I can't live without music to work to, or fire to feed. Harold,
if you asked me to choose between music and fire,

I'd swallow the bird whole and go looking for a light. Don't you know that, Harold? Why do you never ask me about my singing, why do you always hide the matches?

DEFINITE ARTICLE

Here's everything I know about precision:

To say it's the same as accurate is inaccurate. Accurate is the bulb
    orbited by moths—   or rather, the moths themselves,

      even though some never alight. Precise are the petals
threaded to the bulb,   are the early pollinators landing, hoping
to entice the violet flame to open—imprecise is the heart on amateur
      anatomy diagrams, always a bit too far center.

Accuracy begets the calm of the one seated beside the dart board;
the so-few bullseyes,   but the so-little danger (the less precise
                one's location is,
                the calmer they are
                allowed to be).
      The sap
of 1 a.m. air swirling her (which is felt as
                a lack of precision),
                the dull
bar-light glow that lets her watch the thrower, just in case.

      Precision is the flower cut clean off,
the dart flung through stem. Precision
plus accuracy   is the elimination of all flowers
by conscious legislation.

To say words are accurate is unhelpful. To say they are precise is,
admittedly, more accurate, but any understanding
      could just be realignment of the target, after the shot.

Often words don't say what they mean
    or they do say it   but   enact something else entirely.
With the distance of time, accuracy and precision are thrown clear

      from an easy thread, but pull and pull   and the thimbles
          will clatter to the floor near
thumbs still wrapped in their own doing, the moon
          barks on the thimble's metal

like a bomb-sniffing dog.   Night exists to turn the lever
        once farther, to lull the calendar into sleep through which

                it can be carried, time and its mist
        a humid womb the frightened men nightmare about, with knives

        floating, clanging gently against the walls, each other. How
can you spell   the sound of a dog-whistle?   Why
                are so many men   sounding it out?

NOMENCLATURE

A matter of energy conservation. When you see a snake
swallowing an egg whole, assuming it's a bird egg
is rash. It's only rational that it would rain on your day off,
statistically speaking. You can't fault the atmosphere expressing itself.

You have the right to a different path; being not-eaten
isn't a sentence to carrying 70-hour work weeks under your eyes
as your spine Jengas its way to a grave-bed.
Gratefulness needn't take the form of replication, unless
one's just interested in flattery.

Next on Clickbait.com: a video about grandfathers on summits
waiting for mountain climbers to arrive, invoking the new weather
cuffing the climbers on their ears. Someone made a browser app
that changes all instances of *millennials* to *snake people*. The new
economy is just nouns of assemblage: a panoply of politicians,
a larder of ghosts. Do I retweet myself? Very well, then
I retweet myself. I am finite, I contain only so many thoughts.

SELF-PORTRAIT AS MESSENGER APP

Most writing occurs on social media; you have a Facebook self, Twitter self, LinkedIn self, Tinder self. Do you present who you have been or will be—calculate the average projection forward or back among your digital selves, what range their limbs cover, spanning shares, retweets. All of the Great Literature is concerned with the morality of X. Poetry, with a capital P, is concerned with sincerity, in that it's concerned with irony; irony of self in arrangements of discrete recognizable markings, alphabetic formations gathering a fungible storm. Irony is still without clear definition, which is in itself ironic. You have the self you've created in your poems because the poems aren't strictly real. The sum of the self is only what you can fling from where you're standing, what will catch in others' bare, dark branches and will last the season whether wind, whether rain, whether snow or sleet or steel hail. Are you more Hermes or postal service worker?

(I made that up, what Poetry is "concerned" with. I've asked Poetry what's on its mind over and again, and it's only responded with a shudder and a splay, the toppling-over of a bookcase. Am I concerned with poetry? I'm happy that you asked. Have you ever put Greek, Latin, and Old English in a blender and left it running while you were at work? I have; the stanza that my house became changed me. All my locks are opened by tongue now, all the doors are asymmetric. In a breeze, in a breath, the windows drop like anvils.)

IF YOU LIKE THIS

You might like: Morbid curiosity. See also: Consciousness, choice,
psychedelic drugs. If you like food, you might also enjoy air, rely
on water, you're up to six times more likely to have sex before
you turn 80. If you were born in the 90s you're probably alone,
Did You Know you can sell your cultivated loneliness at 2¢/word?
There's always somebody looking for People Like You, versatile
in your utility, ubiquitous in your individualism. Joke: What did one
snowflake say to the other snowflake? Answer: [Say your name here.]

If you like the tone of this poem, thank your right supramarginal gyrus
and Google—though not necessarily in that order. If you like
the sound of your own voice, create Content. If you're unique
in one regard, statistically you're probably not in another
though the research is still out on statistics. Did You Know the odds
of winning the lottery a second time are the same as the first?
Thank your ventromedial prefrontal cortex and indulge.
Related Fractions: 1/2, 8/16, 4/8, 260/520. Joke: What did
the numerator say to the denominator? Answer: I see myself in you.

PUSH

Don't forget: You have 4 events this evening. You have to surface from the bathwaters of sleep and then shower, shuffle your deck of microscopic particles. You have to move cargo from one end of your brain to the other. You have to sing a freeway between bathroom mirror and deadbolt. BREAKING: You have to pick up the kids and reply to your cousin's text and find time to cry inaudibly in a bathroom stall somewhere, preferably while checking email on your phone. You have to cheer, and wrestle, and launder. Reminder: Call Jerry back. Don't forget: 6 deadlines, 3 birthdays and a semiquincentennial celebration to start planning, you have 2 regrets to catalog and 6 weddings and a flu virus that could make a gravestone blanch. Reminder: Take medicine!!! You already picked up the kids, and you have to eat dinner somewhere near where you can refresh the house roster of shampoos, you've got to finish that book on blog posts and that blog post on your first time at a Sox game and your father's coming out, and finally get back to Jerry about that documentary you agreed to watch—you know what, fuck Jerry. Jerry with his World War II histories and 6-watt eyes, his sentences that pounce, fangs out, into the torso of yours. *Well actually*, Jerry, the fish are all dying out because they're trying to get as far away from your voice as they can, swimming deeper and deeper even as evolution sends them a thousand little buzzes of warning. Then they're eaten, eaten by one of those monsters that live down there in the dark, alone and eyeless, until a scale glints with the trace of an alien star, with light impossible, and that *thing*—tooth and bone, no eyes nor basis for understanding the soft glow—lunges, its muscles exacting their solitary purpose, for the kill. And then a silence, holy like death until another message comes shimmering down from the heavens.

DISFLUENCY

When you lose your train of thought, does it crash somewhere?
The woman who answers the pharmacy phone hates me
because of the way I speak (or fail to), the long sentences
and extended syllables I dangle further off the cliff, knowing
a big part of her job is patience, and I hold on saying
so uh and um, the quicksand boot of um, afraid she won't catch me
on her end if I, y'know, leap. If I remain actively engaged uh
in passive voice, do I stutter when I ask you if the um first thing I asked
about the, well, could you repeat that? When you lose the tense
of speech, where does it go? I, and you, and a pizza place.
Would that my larynx could wear a mask, could speak
without the shoddy fence of teeth between us. Yes, I have
taken my irony pills today, wouldn't want to be caught
swinging sincerity around in public.
I've been schooled in the art of knowing, which is to say
saying that I know. Is there a word for two words
back to back, identical but grammatically correct ("You're right, I do
do that," &c.)? I know, y'know; I just want to see if uh
if you do too. If curiosity is a strength, is the asking
of a question a type of flexing? Does speaking in nothing
but rhetorical questions make one an alpha-male, hiding
a hollowness stretched open by a lack of what: a positive
male role model, understanding of the space one
self takes in a grocery aisle, subway car—or, simply, is it jealousy?
Jealousy, the frail ghost that stutter-steps its way past my lips, or
wait no that's fear, fear of public speaking, fear of heights, death or
wait every fear is the fear of death, isn't it? Every empty-calorie
phoneme a stall. Why are we discussing anything else, why wouldn't we
be screaming our fear of death, y'know, every minute of the day?

LIFE HACKS FOR BEING A PERSON

I

Be born screaming, go out
taking in dirt or fire.
Substitute water, accounting for
air at a given altitude, ego,
attitude, whether parent A
was more helicopter or drone,
more corporal punishment or
peaceful protest. Whether parent B
at all. Bring to a rolling boil;
the ingredients will lose their
molecular integrity at
a rate of 18xy, where x
is the barometric pressure
of your childhood comfort-
bubble, and y is the universal constant
of atoms pinballing you toward
something no chance in hell
you can avoid. If a train leaves
for Chicago at 6pm and you're
off at 5, and you're on
it, what are the chances that,
before you fall asleep against
the window and its comet lights
smearing through the rain, a black
hole beyond our mechanical sight
just burped up a star? Solve for
inadequacies (OED definition); show
your work; justify your reasoning;
simplify, simplify, simplify.

II

The rope in the hearse
pulls the same at the port.
Mollify, multiply, ossify.

The law in verse
is the same in the court—
justify, justify, justify.

CROWDFUNDED POEM

I cast a tiny shadow with the lights directly overhead.
I am a known quantity, self-packaged and pre-labeled and consumed
with how to talk to others about my needs and desires, whether a partner
or my stakeholders: the greater community reflected by the sample
size street-block, everyone I could conceivably sell a couch to
on Craigslist or ask to the potluck. I am prepared for you
to evaluate me and find me worthy of a sum you could measure
out to the nearest quarter hour of your shift. Go find me
worthy of some shared extravagance down here, go find me
an extra vacation day or a substitute for parental leave.
Go find me pixie dust, kind gestures to strangers caught on video.
Go find me a college degree without a Theseus string
of monthly installments. The random dispersion of atoms
willfully unaccountable for every action, reaction, that which
causes weather and the fucking in the next apartment over,
the moans that spread on the other side of the shared wall
like a breath you can see in the dead winter, go find me that.

NET WORTH

Let's talk equalities, exchange rates:
There are sixteen pebbles in a rock, three rocks
in a stone, and little to no stones
in a sawbuck. A fist is scarcely adequate
replacement for a heart, regardless of relative size.
Look over there—so *that's* where
the buck stops, where unstoppable force
meets immovable debt. This war
is impressive—you can tell by the gift shop.
Multiply a four-year institution of learning
by its cost-to-benefit ratio, repeat
for the number of American Dreamers
and you've got yourself a reliable
income base (*Solve for "You"*). It's an elite
university, we're an exceptional nation—you can tell
by the incarceration rates, the efficiency
with which we feed bodies into the chipper,
the economy of our languages, recessing.
Look for the littlest portions of self,
snapped down to fit in a headline, the sum of parts
being measured and meted for spices and gold.

OBSERVATION EFFECT

Nothing exists in a vacuum. Schrödinger's dust bunnies cannot be
bought nor sold; if they could vote—they are either abstaining
to make a point or ineligible due to unconfirmed
existence—they would support neither Hoover
nor Bissell because of immigration policies considered harsh or
even murderous (depending on whether we look or turn away).

Something human in the eyes of the doomed cow makes us
reconsider meat, but as drones pepper cities with shrapnel
we keep voting to kill. Cattle conscripted to the business of disappearing.
If we observe ourselves only in the eyes of another, we rely on them
to tell us we're alive. Alive as technically possible, if vying for resources
is living, if the force of your being crumbling another
is how you need to hear your name called.

TRANSITIVE PROPERTIES

It's an utter
failing

of our language that
there's no single

word for the
experience

of listening
to "The Rainbow

Connection."

In 1996

a New Zealand man
held his local

radio station
hostage,

demanded the song
be played for twelve

hours on end, to
tell people how

he felt.

What puts a gun

to another's head,
demands

translation? Demands
understanding—

lovers, dreamers
no more immune

to the sickness
of power, we

have felt
this too, syllables

like valleys pulled
taut in our chests,

the vibration

of string to bone

and where
is all that energy

to go, to
what imperfect

system next: joints,
galaxies,

knowledge.
If death

is a thing,
it is only

what we cannot
say. Everything

else is light
and song.

THE FISHERMAN AND HIS WIFE

"Go to it, then: it is dust already."
—*The Brothers Grimm*

Here is a map made of fire, question-marks of curling flame.

Pull the corner across. Where is the rain? O let it rain, let me
make it rain, answer every query with a trillion utterances of *yes*
or plunks of *no*, the hail to fall like a vowel,
the jawbreaker sweetness of creating silence.

If you ask a tree a question, the wind will answer. Don't be surprised
when the fish answers with only hook and gulp; the question's

curved to puppet the lips, caster interrogating the sea
to extract—what could the black depths show us
that we don't already know about ourselves? A question

infers an answer: a kind of consumption. And that's how we,
as a nation, grow. Every day I answer to the economy, and it asks me
three more questions. Decisions perfumed with meaning,
the placing of that perfume in a box in a bigger box
calculating dimensions of the room, per square foot per
city block, space and limitations and placing a garbage can
in front of the west-facing window so the day deposits there.

Purchasing as an action with an undefined target. To return
control, some agency outside ourselves, to hack the hierarchy
of needs, instead of playing the composition of blood cells
shuffling their boxes until the warehouse shuts down, until the questions
too overwhelm our ability to answer, and we put our hands up,
helpless, a child asking to be picked up and held.

Give us life, and death, and an exclamation point to connect them—
punctuation cocked and ready.

A gun knows only of gun things, do not ask it about return trips.

WHERE FIRE COMES FROM

Necessity is the mother of invention, but the search
is still on for the father. Zeus, having fucked everything,
was a natural suspect, but maybe Adam: overcompensating,
missing rib, the rope of control going slack, hissing
through his hands. The economy was a necessary function
of human advancement and the reality of scarce resources;
when people yell to burn it all down they forget fire too is scarce.

"Not All Fires maim a community!"
Not all fire cleanses, not all floods hit their mark. Not all of us
should be saved. But some do, some should,
and sometimes it's not surprising when a sown seed
becomes a tree that is parched and dry and taps
outside our window with branches sharp as knives.

STRAW POLL

The camel's back broke under worry
and my stress-eating. We are / I am
defined by stuffing, content or lack thereof.
I wash my hands on auto. Check the non-calls,
see that the inbox is still empty and well-dark
and violently open. I throw those few seconds away,
a desert piling up on the other side of the glass.
I am / we are museums of scarecrows, diagnosis
is another word for stitching, calling's the needle
and voice the thread; there is nothing
you cannot become. Just ask for a name.

A new poll suggests 100% of time
is wasted. Then a story about a local woman
arrested for stealing a truck of apples. For dinner
someone will enjoy a steamed crab, its shell
like a bright Gobi dust. At a fundraising dinner
a crab gripped the edge of my plate as if
the claw in a crane game, I wouldn't
eat it, didn't have it in me
to break it, get at its insides, I kept
drawing eyes on the shell, in my mind,
it was watching me, asking how
it came to life, who am I to do
this? I am someone who drew my skin
myself, since I moonlight as a tattoo artist
every third Wednesday of summer months
in odd-numbered years when I feel like it
and Mars is in the House of Crows
where rent is due.

The commercial asks *Who are you*
then suggests three alternatives.

YEAR OF THE LEAST AMONG US

Today is National Pizza-Eating Day, a nice follow-up to yesterday's Hug Your Best Friend Day, as well as the recent National Ginger Day and Day of Reverent, Brief Comic Book Un-Dust-Jacketing.

There is a day of the week for every emotion, an hour for every crisis before the camera crews are called elsewhere. A month for War Holiday I and another for War Remembrance A, a Week of Memory for your favorite cat but also a Week devoted to the unmoving face as seen through lash-strewn tears at the memorial service.

As a matter of survival we developed recognition of patterns, which are nature's foremost hobby. To make a living you are taught to segment markets, you are taught organization, the justification of paragraphs, the predictability of the replication of organ cells.

You have one channel for sports and one channel for food. In this Year of Most, you have a channel for rage and one for worry, for false hope—this is the day of the week for religion, this is the day of the week for lust and rain, this is your day off, this is when you remember your mother, this is the day when you howl, this is the one day of the year when you can leave all the cage doors open, knowing the birds will come back.

ODE TO THE CHARGING CABLE

Persistent whisperer, beginning
of many ends & end
of the diaphanous trek of electricity
through wave & turbine,
fiber & ground & up
through the home's flooring;
yarn-spinner, enabler, life-
preserver in the ocean of codified air
we're apt to drown in; omni-
lingual snake threaded through
bedframe up to my nightstand,
holding steady as if content
to sleep for once, but no—
satellite's floodgate, pipe with no end
you dance within the binary,
the on-off, you eke
motion into the dormant & bray
into the piled minds of AI,
all coiled, conductive, rope
& all the good or evil
one could do with a rope; I
am tethered to the idea of you,
of proximity akin to shelter
or food, & you feed,
blue-lit worm of entropy, mouth
wide, pins of teeth—that's not
fair, parasite is off by direction,
maybe you're a monochrome
Robin Hood, catalyst
& balancer, lightning in need
of no rod, where phone lines
don't grow in the dirt you prosper,
flower & spark in the night,
bioluminesce the faces peering
down, taking you in, from the canteens
of portable batteries
you rise like smoke

decoding a message from beyond—
a loved one's name flashing
on my phone, dead four years, now
calling,
calling,
calling once more.

SYNC

And below the lamp-light moon,
the glinting ocean of grass.

Electric bill unpaid, how the night
comes on slowly, collecting

in unforeseen corners like dust
settling atop the mantel, the chair,

limp hill of shoes, the stairs.
The child next door wails, probably

carrots again—is she always
this loud? The streetlights come on;

within the dense cube of rooms,
feature-sharp and dark, you are alone,

at once. Buzzing, humming outside.
Row of lit windows, a gliding ship

beside you. A figure in the porthole
looks back, returns your expression.

The pilot light clicks on like a universe.
How many things in the home

can whir, can plug and play and
illuminate, frost the apartment walls

with blue light. A world of flame
in a home full of fire extinguishers.

A fan that kneads the two-floored
air of an open stairwell, chugs along.

Outside has assumed a silence wide
as the ocean, as death, echoes of the scorched

earth of building development, and only
now do the streetlights pop

open their memories, sudden blisters.
Across the street, someone has faced

a mirror out of their window. You thank
an attentive God for your reflection.

E PLURIBUS UNUM

I'm jealous of Amherst's Garlic Festival—
all my town has is a Tripe Festival. Entry is mandated
by public code and winners are given spots on city council
though the council never meets. Each member
has the authority of law at all times. Did you know
both spiders and clear water are banned here?
They started painting the smokestacks green
so now everything's fine, only looks like the forest
is on fire. Sure, your sustainability initiative
is great, but what about your social life—have you ever
tried weeping garishly in front of a mirror,
chiming *introvert, introvert?* I've heard that if you shout
introvert! loud enough into social media, the echo will summon
impossible Others, who are one in a million like you. That statistic
is verified; there are three hundred and twenty introverts in America,
and when two find each other
they not only form a sacred bond of friendship
but must then try to kill the other before they
themselves are irrevocably changed—and it's just so hard
to get to know someone, even if it's yourself.

EPITHALAMIUM (II)

At our wedding, your son wore the smallest tuxedo I had
and have, still, ever seen. The tux made him, too, look smaller,
his grin wider than the lapels, a chandelier
overseeing the occasion of his attire.
At the reception he led a trained tiger onto the floor
and the whole room held a reverent silence as it sat beside you,
a familiar. For our honeymoon we were given
an economy of fishing line,
olive trees, stone. We drank coffee that dripped off awnings and when
we found an injured dove on the sand, mended
its pinkened wing. Fashioned a splint while it rustled
and murmured in your grip. In order for a death
to take hold it must be suffused with silence; therefore
our cheating of oblivion with fire, popcorn, sex. Roars,
explosions or applause, of a spontaneous crowd
that wrapped around us
before we thought to question how long a dove would survive
without flight. The mountain gods crowned you
with a diadem of sonnets, the ocean gods struck
the cliffs in anger, jealousy a momentum in search
of something unmovable. The blood
for which the bird's wing pinned to its side,
the fear of its loss,
pounded in our ears, the way our blood
rushes in our children and pushes them on, seeks out
their hands, curls five fingers around a small and frantic heart,
reaches for what is needed, feared, desired,
for what is offered, given, what is refused, what is lost
and not yet lost, and what is curled up in our touch, what is found
and not yet found, where it becomes what is had,
and to have, and to hold.

CARNIVAL

I throw baseballs into the house of mirrors
to see if Speed Pitch works through refraction.
Reflection? I never know; this is why
I stand outside on the dirt path and hurl
four-seamers at the distortions of myself
nanoseconds old, beaming back at me,
smug—a homeowner! In my office, a handsome
bound dictionary, everything in its place: reflection
here, refraction there, all the lights have their own windows
from which they talk to the ends of the street.
What wonder to see through oneself, to pack up
and hit the road when you become opaque,
when the snow sends its emissaries from the north.
Say: Fried dough. Mean: Conduit
for powdered sugar to self, where
are we going, purrs the van, murmur the trucks
whose orange lights make the Self glow,
pale in the way dusk makes pale.
Wear the clown mask, the painted shirt,
the elephant trunk elastic-banded, give up
the corporeal, exist solely (which is
a pun) as idea, move on, page
to page, hearth to hearse, dust to
anything that will cram in the trailer
for the cavernous road ahead. The corn maze
may as well be nothing—which it is, really,
just absence already chosen for you—and how
have so few people taken advantage
of a *maize* pun there? Is it because punning
is reserved for the tilt-a-whirl announcer,
while lack of awareness is the gift
of the Heaven-struck man writhing
on the dust amid the game alley, babbling,
his tongue a channel for something I can't
hear, am not around to hear anyway, and even
then, could not over the mirrors shattering—
I am not my body, I'm just living here.

FORTUNE COOKIE: "OPPORTUNITY WILL KNOCK. WHEN IT DOES, OPEN THE DOOR."

Opportunity cost is described as the value of the next best choice not taken. The road pinned on a map for later, a Tinder box full of options. For most species, sex keeps you in business. For ours, the business of sex is less than mutually beneficial; it's no coincidence people smash champagne bottles on hulls unwillingly bearing the pronoun *she*. This is a horrible way to go about your love life; easy to blame the evolutionary need to spread the genetic code, a game of sexual Telephone. Alpha males will trot out this biological excuse, which has a drunk-with-power logic to it that, apparently, is good enough for many.

The beginning of any venture is historically violent—a smashed bottle, ground broken, a beheading. What does not eat is eaten. Who saw a housecat torn apart by a dog and thought, "*There's* a good socioeconomic model"?

If the sky falls we'll tsk-tsk at our crumpled peach trees, wishing we had gone with a sturdier fruit. You can almost hear the disapproval in the shucking of corn, and we are the least satisfied nation. Mouths open to the sky for rain, or mangoes, or Armageddon and the drumbeats of its collapsing buildings. I believe in every god. This belief is radio, fish hooks cast up and waiting to snag an errant prayer overhead. Divining rod split to sky and soil—we follow whomever feeds us.

I'm staring out of the glass storm door, drawn there by my cat's chirping on the shoe mat interrupting my dinner, and making eye contact with a fox in the front yard. Cat between us, the fox weighing the odds of this undertaking, the roulette table in its mind flashing its colors black, red, black, red. Profit, loss, profit, loss.

Back in the kitchen the fortune cookie sits, intact, waiting for an earthquake or just opposable thumbs, for something or everything to happen, a rupture, opening, consummation. For four sevens on a three-seven slot, the machine to pay out, to avalanche not just to the man who's been squatting at that device since morning, but his neighbors and everyone within arm's reach of the floor.

HOUSING COMPLEX

Picture a body: rooms and storage, picture frames piled in a hall closet.

The body: tired, and tired metaphor of *home*—just a new coat

of paint, a new liver, occupant, receptacle of time and alcohol. His

body above my body, my body bordering their leg, her shoulder, grain

of sand rough dividing us, shared driveway, chest to floor, unlocked

door, tongue knocking, knocking, the feet housed in that which knocks,

steps, the carpet unrolling like a tongue, knocking. I'm sorry

for the distance kept marked with irony—though I'd like

to blame the language, opaque chests

of idioms. It should be enough for me just to point at a thing: rock,

tree, lover, friend. The first time I truly needed language, I lied.

ROUNDING ERROR

Every word stands in, badly, for something;
the thing about euphemisms is exactly
the thing it is, which is to say, isn't.
In euphemisms how can we determine pluralism?
Discrete words of a language—the teeth of
a monster that eats us all (is not
nothing uncountable?)—semantically bleach
for tanning season. Enter a plurality, its ands and buts
and the exact number of years, days, seconds before you die
which hang, a hard math
like a blade over our necks. By concealing
that number, are we not being euphemistic?

Who decided euphemisms are sexual by default?
You might agree if you get your news from sitcoms
that use "poet" to mock a character who bludgeons
their way through a sentence, if you prefer
your plots fill-in-the-blank. If you buy canned laughter
it comes with a free pack of euphemisms, so how are you
not going to write a sitcom? Conveniently adhesive,
these opaque joke-boxes can be laid across a script
easily, thanks to the second gravity: standardization.
Relatability is currency, is ratings-
and share-fodder; discovery sulfurs the Soylent.
Someone somewhere now is convinced gravity's
just a thing we tell ourselves, rounded off to, somewhere
someone now is praying at the church of
the cement mouth, voting at the altar of fixed
and blunt and candied. Somewhere Flat-Earthers
are being promoted to management positions.
The night clutches its stone tooth
between its lips, trying to recall a particular number,
how many inches it's supposed to move that rock,
so bludgeoned by the poets and their metaphors,
away from the Earth this year.

NINTH PLANET

What could a person be looking for—breaking into a UPS Store five miles from home on a cold Sunday night—if not their demons? When the gold and silver run dry, mine for the underworld and what it took from us.

The urge to self-destruct: the echo back from the well, the refrain hung from the inner ear: perfection unattained, there's always something better, says the email headline, and you can have it. The bell cannot ring itself.

For every loss there is an equal and balancing gain, chant the day traders before their ritual. *The oak tree: / not interested / in cherry blossoms*, thinks Bashō.

The reassuring uniformity of car commercials. Nothing so unusual as death could occur in an Audi.

Nothing so unusual as death could be found on that planet with its heart frozen in place, visible from orbit.

The wheel-stops in parking spaces are headstones marking the loss of most sunlight hours. The symmetry of the afterlife mists up from the tar.

You should know who I am, says the purchasing decision. *You* could be anybody, which is what's supposed to make America great. This is a lot of potential to carry in reusable bags; America is a lofty bulk that requires its many to heft it along.

You should know who I am underscores every mass murder, every carefully planned moment of disruption, the *I* phallic and hazy but soon to be distinct, analyzed, coins weighed before being placed over the eyes.

You should know who I am, so I carefully prune my profiles. The universe splays out and offers its soft interior. The ukulele spoons its sour tune for the shy first date. I am planting this flag in a crater to welcome the first visitors.

AN ANSWER

Each box thrums like a buried heart, gives
as the heart gives. Until collapse. Working
the memory of venom from my hands, medallions

of hello, Spring's down payment. Sun ekes out
mist after morning's slap of rain, the beehive

rising to a pitch of *almost*, of fury,
the wait, atoms heated and trying to disperse.
I am dressed as an ineffectual god—colors that claim

no fervor from them, nor invoke the fur of predator.
I am pleased, unnoticed while working.

Only when they're alarmed, if I forget
the smoker, will the stingers dig me. I fight
the suspicion they would steal from me—

not mosquitoes with their derrick forms.
My reflex: swat, and only then consider

the ripples rolling outward from under my palm:
fish tip out of the boiling oceans and drop
into the sky, tugged by the moon's thin line; Nor'easters

stalk the autumn coast, drunk through startled-bare
forests. I savor the thought's little fat on my tongue; I've lost

three summers of weight around the waistline
and I'm not sure I'll get the hang of this. I don't know why
we exist but I know whose hands these are, who I am, I know

everything they touch. In two days I'll open the hives
to find them bare, not even a corpse. Teeth picked clean.

I see rivers boil under the flowers they ferry, bees plunging toward
those petals to drown in the acid. And how could they
be saved? Today I do nothing but watch them ease back

into the rainless sky, un-disappeared, the mass of them hovering
like an empty thought bubble, or at least, empty of words

known to me. Each a curled letter, each its own striped flag.

OCCUPATIONAL HAZARD

The heart that fed was user error. Hearts were not designed
to do this, but to store grain
and buoy their chassis, to pump   and thunder
and moan against the frame. Wherefore the rooms

tacked on, guest spaces spooled together
with something like a moat,   who taught us
to love others in our own space? The heavy linework

of the late artist is attributed to an indulgent heart,
          a pet at home   sprawling out on the hearth.
Psychologists wearing muted suits, furrowed ties, prodding a diagram
on the wall and clearing their throats

like the one-TWO of a magazine clip entering its place of worship.
                    Televangelists close their eyes, buzz, tongues
lolling, fattening in their own charged juices; each   vocation
          a wrecking ball into the world of those   who wish
to live quietly. Some choose to consume the heart before it snaps

off the bough and forces them into action, to pick it up and rub it
on their shirtsleeve as if to confirm ripeness

by denying the dirt it sprang from   agency over the taste.
I can't be trusted   with my own heart,
nor can it be trusted alone. Hence the feasting,

organic disposal of evidence. Replication of that hollow
echoing out from cupped hands: stadiums, mausoleums,
all that is built to satisfy a future need. They erect the new world

on top of this one, one apartment complex, one statue
at a time.   Cradles, two Earths. A fear of love so complete
we'd eat the world away to nothing if it were given to us
          to consume.

NOTES

Passages of the preceding poems, often in italics, are taken from/in reference to the following sources:

Associated Press: "Man Takes Hostage, Wants Muppet Song Played for 12 Hours," March 22, 1996 ("Transitive Properties")

Bashō, as translated by Hass ("Ninth Planet")

Everclear, "I Will Buy You a New Life" ("Music Video")

Huffington Post: "A New Gun Folds Up to Look Just Like a Smartphone," March 30, 2016 ("A New Gun Folds Up to Look Just Like a Smartphone")

Nat King Cole, "It's Only a Paper Moon" ("T-Rex")

Pablo Neruda, *Book of Questions*, English translation by William O'Daly ("A Question")

Percy Bysshe Shelley, "Ozymandias" ("Occupational Hazard")

~

The first part of the "Do I retweet myself?" passage in "Nomenclature" is borrowed from a tweet by *Kenyon Review* on 9/24/15.

"A New Gun Folds Up To Look Just Like a Smartphone" owes a debt of gratitude to Karen Skolfield as well as a psychic debt to Vievee Francis.

Italics in "I Hate The Weather Channel" were all taken from the weather.com homepage over the course of several weeks in 2013.

ACKNOWLEDGEMENTS

Many thanks to the editors and staff of the following journals in which some of the poems in this collection, sometimes in different forms, first appeared:

The Adroit Journal: "An Answer" (published as "Beekeeper's Veil")
The Awl: "A New Gun Folds Up To Look Just Like a Smartphone"
Baltimore Review: "Self-Portrait with Oncoming Storm"
Blackbird: "Nothing But," "Ninth Planet"
Booth: "Music Video"
Carolina Quarterly: "Carnival," "Straw Poll" (published as "Carnival Mask" and "The Word Worried is the Word Straw")
Diode: "A Question"
Fugue: "Definite Article"
Gold Wake Live: "Crowdfunded Poem," "Push"
inter/rupture: "Net Worth"
Last Exit: "The First Technology"
The Kenyon Review: "Customer Loyalty Program"
Muzzle Magazine: "De Toros"
Southern Humanities Review: "Epithalamium"
Superstition Review: "Housing Complex," "If You Like This" (published as "If You Like This Poem"), "Occupational Hazard"
Waxwing: "T-Rex" (published as "T-Rex Mask")
Zone 3: "Audit"

Thank you to everyone who has supported me or my poems along the way: editors, readers, friends, family, and the Asheville, Boston, and Manchester literary communities.

Special thanks to Aaron Alford, Michael Bazzett, Eduardo C. Corral, Mckendy Fils-Aime, Lockie Hunter & Jeff Davis, Shelley Girdner, Peter Kispert, Lynn Melnick, Jordan Rice, David Rivard, Sean Shearer and everyone at the 2017 BOAAT Writer's Retreat, Allison Singer, Karen

Skolfield, Rob Stapleton, Hannah Stephenson, Michelle Turner, and Dillon J. Welch, without any of whom this book would not exist. I'm eternally grateful for their friendship, time, care, and attention to my work.

Thanks to the North Carolina Arts Council, Avery County, Asheville Area Arts Council, Toe River Arts Council, and the Madison County Arts Council for their Regional Artist Project Grant support during the making of this book.

Thanks to Kyle and Nick for believing in my words, and to the whole Gold Wake team for helping me bring this book into the world.

And to Catherine for making every day of my life better, for her endless love, support, and willingness to put up with my bad jokes. You and me vs. the world.

ABOUT GOLD WAKE PRESS

Gold Wake Press, an independent publisher, is curated by Nick Courtright and Kyle McCord. All Gold Wake titles are available at amazon.com, barnesandnoble.com, and via order from your local bookstore. Learn more at goldwake.com.

Recent Titles:

Dana Diehl and Melissa Goodrich's *The Classroom*
Sarah Strickley's *Fall Together*
Andy Briseño's *Down and Out*
Talia Bloch's *Inheritance*
Eileen G'Sell's *Life After Rugby*
Erin Stalcup's *Every Living Species*
Glenn Shaheen's *Carnivalia*
Frances Cannon's *The High and Lows of Shapeshift Ma and Big-Little Frank*
Justin Bigos' *Mad River*
Kelly Magee's *The Neighborhood*
Kyle Flak's *I Am Sorry for Everything in the Whole Entire Universe*
David Wojciechowski's *Dreams I Never Told You & Letters I Never Sent*
Keith Montesano's *Housefire Elegies*
Mary Quade's *Local Extinctions*
Adam Crittenden's *Blood Eagle*
Lesley Jenike's *Holy Island*
Mary Buchinger Bodwell's *Aerialist*
Becca J. R. Lachman's *Other Acreage*
Joshua Butts' *New to the Lost Coast*
Tasha Cotter's *Some Churches*
Hannah Stephenson's *In the Kettle, the Shriek*
Nick Courtright's *Let There Be Light*
Kyle McCord's *You Are Indeed an Elk, but This Is Not the Forest You Were Born to Graze*

ABOUT BRANDON AMICO

Brandon Amico is the recipient of a North Carolina Arts Council Regional Artist Grant and the Hoepfner Literary Award for poetry, awarded by *Southern Humanities Review*. His poetry has appeared in journals including *The Adroit Journal, Blackbird, Booth, The Cincinnati Review, Diode, Hayden's Ferry Review, Hunger Mountain, Kenyon Review, New Ohio Review, Sixth Finch, Slice, Waxwing, and Verse Daily*, and his book reviews have been featured by *32 Poems, AGNI Online, The Los Angeles Review, Mid-American Review*, and *The Rumpus*.